The Drowning of
the Ego

Vanshika Dubey

BookLeaf
Publishing

India | USA | UK

Presentation by *BookLeaf Publishing*

Web: www.bookleafpub.com

E-mail: info@bookleafpub.com

ISBN: 9789363313972

First edition 2024

*For my parents and my brother, who have
always encouraged me to write*

ACKNOWLEDGEMENT

Any written piece is a culmination of experiences, dreams and encouragements. To leave the skin of a person and seep into the skin of the character through whose eyes one wants to view the world, one must be mindful of keeping the text real enough to be relatable. I do not know to what extent I have succeeded in this endeavor, however, whatever I have thus produced would not have been possible without the support of my mother who always encouraged me to hone my skills (which, in her loving eyes, have existed in abundance). Having poured words on paper, one also seeks an unbiased review. I had that in the form of my brother who minced no words in telling me what he felt about it. Through his reviews, over the years, I have learned how to use criticism to better oneself. Having said that, he has been the biggest champion of my artistic pursuits and often tells me to listen to everything but rationalize it through your own knowledge. Last, but not the least, I thank my father who has supported my every dream and has taught me to find beauty in life.

PREFACE

I always wanted the world. I walked on the path of my stern principles and left behind those who could not catch up. I was an old lady at first and grew younger as the years passed until I was transformed into a blubbering baby. I understood people very well. The person I saw when I first met them was accurately understood by me. Yet, the more I spoke to them, the less I understood, as my mind was tarnished by my own emotions. Coaxed and thrown out from the womb of comfort, I was caged in overthinking which churned out bleakness.

Disclaimer
This is purely a work of fiction.

You are not at home and you can say it twice

Those **hours** of worry
That culminate
Beyond a single sorry

And here I am
Just another Jane
To mule across my grades
And hence, a burden become

Only, **I did not know it yet**

I did not know
the financials
That gave me all the vigor
I did not see
the worry beneath
The hearts that I punished for my selfish
frustration

But there I was
The baby girl
Who lived a movie dream
And jarred by reality

She screamed

and screamed

and screamed

For all my life I had only known
Textbook examination
But all too soon
I had to grow that adult sneaky bone

As we crossed the country
To reach
The palace that had tried
My sanity
Before I even breached
the grand wall of books that made its concrete

They were all worried
(*Of course family*)
For abandoning me in the wild
And I
I was living the college dream
To be out there
To be seen

I did some prep
Chopped my braid,
Went on a clothing quest (*an expensive one*)

But all my new bulkiness
Held me back
From the confidence I was used to flaunt

The rooms were big
In a city as grand
And decorated with dreams
Old and young, strung along
In like flashy jeans

A newer vibe is what I need
Is what I thought I knew
And ungraciously I chose to forget
All the thoughts I knew

This high was what they feared
(*Of course family*)

They feared the snarky influence
Their dearth would slowly grow
They feared the wavery mind I had
fickleness un-shrewd
(the dangerous kind)

We were all silent and free
The toddlers
Out for blood
From a variety
Born of diversity

Of Society
Singled out
To once again play
That game called competition

Some were kings and some paupers
And the difference in groups was established
Only I was not aware
That I too had to be either one

Punctuality, food
Tidiness, mood

All in a single cube
Twisted across the axis
By fate
Seemingly, Smilingly
fighting for single victories
Every day

Yes, we were all babes
We were all wolves
We were roses
Also thorns but
Only for the other's foot

No damage yet

Yet there were no damages to the other

After all,
Who knows of such things
Only damages to the self
Pinch

And so began the divorce
From childhood teachings
And the mind only accepted
Contradictions that always felt
mellow to the ear

And I could slowly see
Groups
Carving themselves out
And I could only feel
Panic
And teenage loneliness

I thought of the friends I had in Heaven
When we had uniforms
Laughter and not the ugly formality
And exchanged glances
For there were never these many doors to
whisper behind my back
These many walls to overhear
These many eyes that had not seen
My personality
Which, as I grew
To hate

All this was bubbling behind
Laughter
Mine and theirs'

There was so much going around
With teachers and seniors and studies
But what I chose to make loom
Defined me
And the negativities that bloomed
Were born of that choice, a mistake
The uncalculated nuances
Of algorithmic friendships

I was searching for something
Badly, blindly
To guide me through these dimming lights
Of what was understandable
And it took a while (*looking back*)
To realize
It was Mother.

They knew it would be so
(*of course, family*)
And in retrospect- thus the old soul spoke:

En Garde!
Dear Eyes
En Garde!

Alas!
Even as a headache stretched my composure
such piercing mute moments did not stop
My eyes from roaring

Fragments of tears that the soul cried
Of snubs that ruffled the neat creases
Of pretentious dyes
Pragmatic, my mind, threw reasons
For such affections to subside
But all these senses involved
Were never friends

And ever the wagging tongue
Threw away keys which locked all secrets
I was taught to guard
We were never one being
From the start
Of this anticipated journey
And each paid dearly for their betrayal

Trust was the first step to love
Was the last step to love
Was the stepping stone to hate…

BILLY AND FANNY

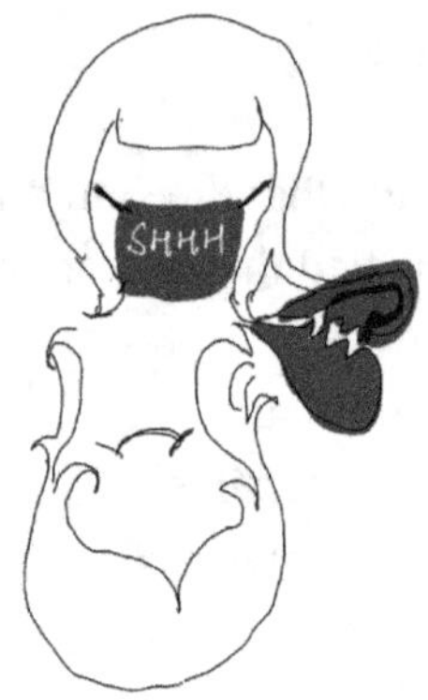

Fanny was the one I saw
First
Thought she would like it too
If she could find her first friend
soon

Oh she did! Did she too?
No, not me, she wanted someone cooler.

She realised though
That first day
We were the only ones
So we made our way downstairs to the mess
To eat together
Talk (*tolerate*)
Discuss five years

But she had the constant smirk-
'Isn't she a fool?'
Was I?
Too OPEN? Too HAPPY? Too SILLY?
What if I had reserved my mind
No nervous giggle
Not thinking she could not be mean without
reason.

She listened with the air of a patient saint
I was patient too
Waiting her rudeness out
Thought, maybe I thought too much
Thought too little
Was too much

I was not at home
And I forgot
These tense moments would not just pass
Opinions being created
Were *permanent*
Fodder for thoughts of those who had not met
me
To paint my character

And every word I spoke
Was scaled
'Isn't she a fool?'

Was I?
Too FRIENDLY? Tried too HARD?
Was I?
As I should have not been?

Billy, I saw next
She was perfect
Warm and friendly and kind
And I knew
Many warm hugs would be exchanged

I saw her in the room
She shared with Fanny
I thought she was the best
The *funniest*
The nicest
Darling.

We would soon be sisters,
And that evening
I knew it in that room.

"Do you like studying history?"
Asked she, with an eager smile
I nodded enthusiastically
"I hate it!"
I laughed.
"But do you like to read?"
Asked she, with a smiling side-eye.

I nodded enthusiastically
"*I don't!*"
I laughed.
"*Where do you live?*"
Asked I
Wanting to know more,
"*Do you know this place x?*"
"*Yes!*" I smiled
"*Well, I don't live there!*"
I laughed. "*Where then?*"
"*Two hours further.*"
And beside me, I saw Fanny
Enjoying with us
And Billy linked her with me in that moment

This trio was the first hope I had seen
Since heaven.
Though Fanny was a tough nut to crack
But time and patience
Would cure all hestiations.

And that night I went to sleep
With a smile on my face.
There were souls around
Outside
Who I was eager to meet again the next day.

ROOMMATE

Something about her struck me... different
The big tall girl in pink
Who sat behind me
Laughing at herself about talking too much
"*Maybe that's her*", I whispered to Billy
The girl who's going to be my roommate

The big tall girl in pink
She seemed confident
Ready to take on challenges
With fun

She seemed
Not lost
Like she had a map
To weave around the *tangled web*
Of early relationships
Maybe she would
Teach me as she went about
Molding life

So I paused
Waited for an intuition
And coincidentally
Found myself in a situation

Of a lift full of people and her

I waited for that initial look
The hesitant expression
Exchanged before smiles took
Over the judgmental silence.

It did not come
Even as the crowd thinned
It seemed
She had made up her mind
Already about me
And remembering my intuition
Hope became dread
Maybe she would
Treat me like that
With contempt (without knowledge).
And I began hating the idea of her

There was a blue-eyed boy
A senior
To whom she was *breathlessly* talking
His girl next to him
Took a liking
To asking her the allotted hostel room

And I prayed with open eyes
And a stoic face
That manifestation had a refund policy

"*Five forty-two*"
The number matched
And I found myself speaking
"*Hey! I'm glad*"
She spared me a look then
While I welcomed her
to the room I lived in.

There was to be an *invader* in my home
Not an ally no friend
A foe
Stronger I would rise to the challenge
Passive aggression? I could do that
I had grown up with aunts
Hinting crap at my mother

She spoke to me
Letting me know she had to
There was nothing in the world she could do
Including giving friendliness a chance.

She was to check in a little late
A few months hence
When her parents returned to stay
From their business
Her little brother, you see, needed her
And she would commute
Everyday

Through the rain and dirt
For him.

I was relieved
It would give me time to stitch
Closer bonds around me
Time, she would miss
ignorantly hating me
I would take care of me.

That night there was an issue
The walls leaked
Water
For once not secrets
And my habitat
Was a patient
There were some repairs to be made
So I called her

No 'hello'

So I texted

No reply

So I waited….

The black in the sky
Kissed orange

And thus began
The *first* day
Of every issue I would ever have
For the next few years.

That first day
I would forever remember
I realised two things
She was determined to dislike
The sight
Of the girl, she was stuck with (me)
And number two
I was in deep trouble with my future (more on
that later).

The girl in pink
Became stronger like a rash
That is given scratchy attention
Not even polite
She had that look
Like I was puke
Though she muttered impatient nothings
so as to deflect
Any confrontation
A direct retaliation could have

I began to think
Something was wrong with me

Both her and Fanny
Seemed to have similar thinking
Where salutations with me were concerned

I did try
To keep up the conversation
"I called you last night," I said
(smile smile)
"I know"
(roll of the eye)
"well" I hesitated
"I would have picked up," she stated
"I was free but did not feel
The want for small talk" (a little laugh)
I gaslighted myself
Telling myself not to be too harsh
My opinions tended to be permanent
And I did not want
Early days to be dented
With my short temper.

My first mistake with her
Came immediately afterward
As I introduced her
To Billy and Fanny
And through them
She began the balancing act
With all my friends
While keeping an eye

On the glam gang
Thinking she could sankritse
Herself into someone she was not.

As I sat next to her
That first day
I saw her hesitate
On the simplest of questions.
Someone asked her what her dad did
She said he was an officer all grand
Said her boyfriend was from the first family
Of the city she lived in
Said she was out all night, all busy
Had a guy friend taking her out
He had a tattoo
Of the vibrations of her recorded message
saying *"I love you"*.
And as we soaked it up
Some ears perked
With interest resonating with the delicious
possibility of a lie
Ah! The doubt
Was such a topic
Food for gossip
A trap for her was planned out
The people she wanted to like
Would soon strip her paint
That she used
To cover up her complex.

"I forgot your name" I said
"Ken" She said
Made me want to giggle
"Where is your barbie?"
She looked confused
"Anyway, could you add me to the class group?"
Add Ken to the group, I wrote with flourish
This tickled Billy
"Who's Ken?"
"Why, her of course", pointed I
"Did you hear Ken? She said Kailey,"
Said Billy laughing Silly
Laughter and joy
Is what I felt
And thought it a wonderful Ice breaker

Though Kailey remained quiet
Barely polite
Through a tight smile
Irritation though
Hooded her eyes
With shadows of resistance
To positivity.

And she stuck her claw on Fanny
Who was delighted
At the prospect of shared nonchalance
All acted

With someone
To play it out
The subtly terrible seclusion
Showing how much she doesn't care.
Except she did
Which was a flaw
In someone
Throwing so many stones
With such passion.

With Fanny the thing was
It wasn't a clear snap
She wanted friends
Didn't want to show it though
She wanted connection
But she was 'OH-SO-FINE WITHOUT IT'
At least that's what she showed

So they had this friendship that lasted a week
Weak for no bond
From Kailey the freak
Weak for no bond
From the pretentious geek.

Billy was fine
She was kind
No power play
All divine
And among the din

It seemed I found my kin
Nice was perfect
In that palace of unkind.
Maybe they were just early days
But her aura attracted
Sisterhood out of me
Someone to look up to
Someone *real.*

So when we went back
From college to the hostel
The next few hours
Would span out predictably
If Billy was there
We would walk back, eat
Come back together
study
Without Billy
Fanny
Enjoyed leaving me
Acting as if she forgot
Everyday because her thoughts
Just couldn't seem to find me in them
And Kailey just went with the flow
Wicked delight for
Days when the permutation set me aside

Giggle giggle
We forgot

Giggle giggle
You're only an afterthought

Giggle giggle
Don't take offence

Giggle giggle
We don't need to make amends

Giggle giggle
Poor girl

Giggle giggle
We keep forgetting her

Giggle giggle
Let's see if she dares

Stand up for herself
Leaving herself with fewer friends, bare
Ego and power play
Is a wonderful game
When the majority is on your side
Stood up against
Weak-spirited lost fools who were earlier
carefree bold
Now live in a servile mode
Giggle giggle

The test is on
Giggle giggle
We have already won.

And these politics
Were broadcasted
Well at night
During din-din- as Kailey called it
That way they were all evened up in their rooms
Met each other every day
Their doors opened up to face each other.
And this game
They had commonly arranged to play
Against me, not daring to stand up and say
She wants to sit with us
Let's call her
'No, if we holler
Her mind will twist itself
In giving her respect
Which she doesn't deserve'

And I
strike through
I did not deserve
Their respect
If I could not respect myself

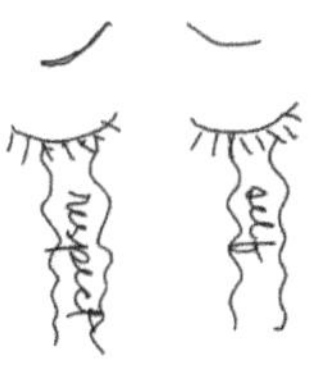

And so the mess table was laid
With six chairs

So declared
Billy and Fanny
Tanya and Olive
Esha and Deedee
With permanent shares
And now and then
Hanging on to them
Were attachments
from other groups
Who sat with them
if they managed to match the time

So far so not good
But I could only afford
So many affronted feelings.

Mess Table Politics

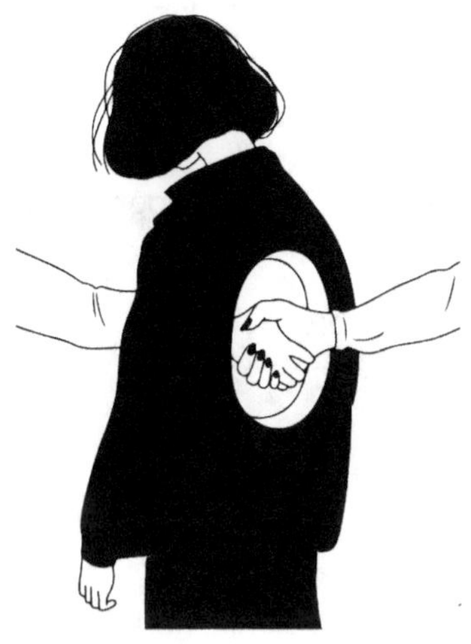

It began this way-
"We forgot to call"
"Can't wait for you"
"That's your job."

I chose some birds to flock with
Huddle together
Protected
But I stood out- night against day
Our feathers couldn't find common colours
With which to paint friendship (gel with)

My night was at its darkest,
I could see;
To the beauty of the dark,
 I was blinded.

Hush! Hush!
Went the footsteps past my door
Downstairs, no talk
Just agree to ignore
'*She's not with us! She's such a bore!*'

The odd one has no ties
Phoebe was all a lie

And all across were bulbs in minds
With a pinch of a yearning to be kind
To their decisions,
They liked, some strange company some silly
time
But (and yet again! But!)
Ignorant fun is to be frowned upon
It takes a while I suppose
Cowardice comes in every form.

So, trailing I went
And was greeted with an 'oOpPs'
Smirks, glances, side eyes, lashing flutters
Some couldn't look up
Some shrugged

Helpless, I suppose
To the majority's word ((less) orders)

"Could you get me some extra gravy?"
"Some extra salt?"
"Some extra-"
Maybe (no!)
"Of course!"

I dared not
Give voice to the knife within
Sigh! and glare and roll my eyes and grunt
Not retaliating was lesson one
I had to spend five years in that dorm
And cowardice comes in every form.

They reflected social life
Those mess tables
Which were of two kinds
One HUGE
To host sixteen
Fencing the right-hand section
And then nuggets splattered all across
Neat tables of four
Though chairs were dragged (squeak!)
To jumble up those numbers

And enter I would
And there they would be

Sixteen and full
Six culprits (The seventh had not yet arrived)
And rest- innocent bystanders
Who loved the daily drama
Then there were two
Who initially made a show
Of eating together- alone (nugget)
And claimed they were not at ease
With the crowd that gathered
To eat.

It *hurt*! It *hurt*! It *hurt*!

Breakfast- Lunch- Dinner

It *hurt*!

Silly me- all I had to do was to stop caring
But (But! But! But!)
What of ostracism? Of loneliness?
Five years without
No family
A love drought.

Yet, I would sit
There with them, hoping to fit in.

"Do we HAVE to wait for you?"
Asked the one with a horrid expression and
syrupy voice (Fanny).
"No," I mumbled, a weak smile

Try as I might
I knew the slap I felt
Echoed in an ascending scream
Through the muscles of my face.
And they saw this, their sorry expression
showed
And they liked it, everyday actions showed

It had never been so difficult before
Back in heaven.

So I knew what I had to do
Solve this puzzle and put a stop
To this daily beating
I clocked my arrival every day
figured out the time,
Though the challenge lay
In keeping my desperation inconspicuous

Early I came
I waited for them to come
I was snubbed once or twice
For when I sat first
The table was shifted to another by that one girl
(Olivia)
And the rest followed

Late I came
I ate so fast

Guinea's bowed
And patted myself when I realized I could get up
with them
Every once in a while there would be a girl
There instead of me
And I took solace in that fact.

Early, I came
Eventually
Acceptance began blossoming
And I worshipped the alters of initiators
To sit with the gang
Was royalty

Late, I came
I was invited
As I got up with them
For outside walks
For laughter
For talks

And I began
Losing myself in the college dream
In the friendships had just begun

All it cost me was my backbone.

There were groups budding all around
With envious conviction

At the corner, I saw it come together
Common cash creating 'class'.
Their pinky liked to shy away from touching a
ladle or handle
Their skin, so polished, I saw myself reflected
Bathed in insecurity
I saw their finger so perfect could have been
painted
And postures that only liked company
Of attention from afar.

Then there were some girls who sat, united by a
common tongue
They seemed to have found
An easy algorithm for homesickness.
But (**but**!) my words were not so unique
To be powerful enough to segregate
Comfort and Cunning.
Danger! All around me

Who I chose
Would define my life
In these formative years
And so the middle path (the best route)
Was the largest pack
Diluted enough to not stand out
Wash out
Disappear. (something positive)

Too **different**

Too different I was
All awkwardly, not charming
And my speech betrayed only the silliness that
came out at home
No maturity, no education
Just silliness embossing nervous energy

And I chose to suppress
My true quirky self
Thought I had to say- things that most lived
The life at home
The school activities
The conversations with friends
The locality I live in
Were all painted over
With the mediocrity of pretention
I was too afraid, *too afraid* to be me
The first month I learnt
It was not a good thing to be
'Me' had to change
If I had to survive among other wolves.

And yet, I saw this one lone wolf
Who chose a new pack every day
Never accepted one
Was never accepted in return
She was the dork

Someone to be laughed at
Someone apart
(*'A kindred soul? I do not know. What if I look
too closely and see me, as she is?
Someone to laugh at?
Someone apart?*)

Funny thing
In heaven I too did not have
A pack
Just friends
Who were me and mine
Who cared about the world
When five of us could be
Perfect without it?
But there was not one, not one, nada
As weeks bled
Away with my dignity
The mind lost
Connection to the soul.

I was awful
I was not enough
I chose not to be
My mistake
I did not like myself
Was not brave enough to love
The person my parents raised

All I could love
Was the idea of acceptance
I was awful
I was not enough
To be a friend
To anyone else
in that atmosphere (WORD!)
When I could not even be an acquaintance of my
own.

The First Call

"*Mum?*"
Am I bad?
Am I too much
Not enough?

"*Mum?*"
Am I young?
Amongst the grown-ups having fun?

"*Mum?*"
Have I not learned?
To smile without permission?

"*Mum?*
Am I too much of a coward
About everything in any world?

"*Mum?*"
Why can't I be
Perfect?

"*Mum?*"
Is it not okay for your words?
To be sought for help

Remain traditional amongst the chaos

" ***Mum***?"

My friends say
I am irritating, annoying
Mum?
How do I find out how common that saying is?

" ***Mum***?"

Can't I go?
Start over again?
These past months

" ***Mum***?"

Can I come home?
To magic, it's tragic
How I still think of it

What if I'm not strong enough
Not tough
Too smooth
To handle rough
Or am I too rough?
Too unskilled
To seem smooth?

Where is the booth

That I can use to call
Whoever has the answers
If you don't

Maybe it is all well
My experiences will cure
My view of myself as a child
Everything will be for the better
If I treat it so

Yes to the reality
That only my parents think I light up the room
And the tragedy is I ever thought two people
thinking so
Were not enough
While they were more
That one could ever hope

For; Yet, I forgot
The only validation I needed
Were those two.
All I need to do is endure
Survive the nonsensical ego deals

For the world around me
Probably, these incidences were laughingly
brushed aside
Yet as they happen,
I wonder if they know

My reality gets limited to them.
And I am the fault
For letting it grow
That horrible mould
Into something that could eclipse
My hold
On m y s   e   l   f

PICNIC

The prologue is such
Sometimes after hell has broken lose
And one has walked through its fiery trials
With a steadily beating heart
There is a picnic reward in response to a call
Of a respite to the mind
Freedom across the walls

Now dear reader
As I break the fourth wall
Listen to the fun
Through a nerd's *crazy* drawl

There is nothing risque about innocent bunking
Stylish escapades, across illusion of money trials
Probably there are those who get truly crazy
Jump the wall, burn all quals
And let surrender to experience

Not experience to mould as per personal
hesitation.

Sigh! I am of the quieter kind
My craziness is different
More profound, changeling that I am

One day, acrophobic me went TREKKING
As a respite from the stress all around
As I neared the cliff, my confidence dwindled
And that was when I experienced, the love of
friends
Who then hesitated, not irritated
About my many fears

Oh, **joy**! I tiptoed through the edge of fear
There was a glaring sun
Affecting those who could think through a lack
of adrenaline
This calmness has many flaws
It opens one to reality
Not protected by the mind's cage
Concentrating on not falling
For the fear of flying forever

I have around me
Cheering me on
My friends who teased me and eased me
Through this journey of flaws

Where they shone in perfection

Kiss the love
When thanking god
Sometimes such trauma can flush out well
Negative influence birthed by personal
insecurities

There is something wicked
About beaches
Barefoot, tickled, through the waves of sand
And the sea pastes out garments to every curve
But there is no shame
In such exposure
Joy resounds
The body is free
Of expectations
Beyond the volleyball
The mind never catches the fever

And, oh dear friends
I miss our waves
The ones that tucked us
Into second-long pauses of glee
Repeatedly
Laughter was unabashedly let free
And our voices from across the country
Sang the tune of harmony
The melody of which sings to me

Through photo treats

Hold my hand
The friendly one
The other one is meant for caution
That was the only crutch

As I **bled** away my social pretenses

 And gave in to every raw thought
The worst form of nudity
Perfectly socially acceptable
Imperfect in its very existence

And how protected they let me be
They let me stay
Away in solace
From communications better suited for our age
Coddled me, pampered
And we acted out our roles well defined
That we had created
Hush now! Every comfort demands payment
And when comfort raises its invoices
They are always **hefty**…

The Worst of Humanity

Beaming smiles greeted me
As the girls with shy pinkies
Spoke to me and made my day
Suddenly, I feel like
I've moved up the food chain

They do smile
And ask me why
I remain close to only a few
I wonder why
They've deigned this way today

A "*Hi!*" sends me quietly blushing
And feel examined
Under the eyes of teachers, I have not paid
They are suddenly quite interested
In knowing of my life

Suddenly, I realise it's not one
But plenty
And people have keen eyes
And more time
That I ever imagined
They know the clothes
From Monday to **Monday**

Of people
And they have them rated
Not liked, berated
Desirability is defined
Through their definition

My head is swimming
In emotions, I do not want to own
I feel like I have conquered
Everything Vogue

And one of them nonchalantly brings up
"*Kailey*", the not so big of a mystery
There is a strange rumour circulating
Her self-proclaimed status
Of dating a social media celebrity
"*Her?*" unbelievable!
And I feel strangely protective
Of somebody I share a room with

Before my eyes, they transform into vultures
The kind you have to hunt
For self-preservation
A bunch of girls egged on by the boys
Who as usual are all aligned
And pride themselves and getting girls to play
Politics for their boredom (the fools!)

"*When does she sleep?*"

I feel weird and a little- *"er..."*
 All I can gather
Is the scent of something fishy
Then suddenly
The colonial crowd before me
Grows bolder (or determined- it's difficult to
discern)
"Did you see her stories?"
"My world! A girl so boring-
Cannot (does not deserve to)
Afford to be wooed!"
"Poor girl- she is deluded,
Her beau exists in the fantasies of her head
Does she talk to him late at night
Dear Annie- **will you be our little spy**?"
"Will you be our little spy?"
"Will you be our little spy?"
"Will you be our little--"

"Why?!" I am aghast
How blasphemous
Of the world at large
They want me to peep into her phone
And check for an iota of truth
In Kailey's words

They are suddenly at it
Telling me the things she says
About my irritating being

And for once I school my hurt
Kailey, of course, must be heard
But to do what they want of me
Was worse than insanity
So I decided, I must communicate with
The roommate I hate

HI KAILEY

There was not much I had to say
To Kailey who was easily swayed
By her nasty moods
And her deluded vigour
She wanted so bad to be worshipped
Like an influencer

She was an owl
In her sleep cycle
She cried foul
When questioned about her racist blabber
She wagged her tail at money's trail
And her attitude, that she thought cool
Was a *dysfunctional* muck of insecurity

Now dear reader
You may wonder what
She did to me
For this kind of description
"*Just wait*" will be my genius advice
For all that is to come, this is nice

"*Hi Kailey!*" I said daily
(On a side note, this rhyme was unintentional)
Kailey had her earphones on

She could hear through the music passing
The cheap wires amassing
Music that constituted her only thoughts
That she could hear me
I could tell
(She would confess,
Later, during our *friendship spell*)
She continued munching
On her heart attack
And would go her own way
If I attempted at
Asking any further questions

I felt like a dog
Trying to get
Her master's attention
I too was searching for comfort
(There is none beyond childhood)

"Hi Kailey"
I said that day
And she ignored
My voice as usual
But that day I was on a mission
I was immersed in the will to be moral
(A fool's endeavor)

"They are asking about your paramour?
Your *"poochie-poochie"*

That you posted about
Meeting last night
Going on a drive
Did you really? Is what I've been asked
Please be careful
-**P-r-e-d-a-t-o-r-s**- are on the prowl

That caught her attention and
She left suddenly with a frown
I wondered at it and soon
Went to the corridor, attracted by snorts
I saw her with one of them
They sobered up
As I crossed
And laughter resumed
 Behind my back
I hated myself then
For trying to help
Because it seemed like all evil was
Between beings from hell, amongst themselves

So I waited with a baited breath
Kept mum about what I could have further said
And one day
They started shooting
Comments about every aspect of her being
Her weight (too bulky)
Her clothes (too ugly)

Her words (all garbled)
Her stance (**so awful**)
Every bulky bullied girl
Specs, braces, chubby curves
From all pop culture references
Dissolved into a common pool of angst
Personified in real life Kailey

To see someone sob
From the only approval she sought
Not from a boyfriend but from a clique
She prayed before in inferiority
And to see a soul crushed
Through *leaking* eyes
There was no guise
Inside
The four walls within which she lived and hide
Her pride
Already an ailing patient
Was sent to the afterlife

Funnily enough, a phenomenon was seen
As the university gossip social media page
Began starring
Kailey as the chosen pig (for slaughter)
Sympathy existed in the world knowing
The immorality was unbecoming
But jabs on a person
No matter how evil

If presented with sufficient humour
Create a sliver of excusable acceptance
Greedily devoured and repeated aplenty
Social media enthusiasts exist
In a life of moral lectures
Covering up what's evil but funny

Humour if done well
Can stamp the most atrocious things
With approval
No matter how cruel no matter how mean
It's a game then
To repeat it first
To the next person who hasn't heard
The latest punchline
And the headline is based on a false rumour
Uneducated journalists swimming in
incompetence
Spinning tales through chinese whispers

Suddenly Kailey was
Someone who unclothed
Loved to send her snaps
To whoever was willing to pay
Her greed was never-ending
And she could do anything (anything!) for
money

To see her crushed
Everyday
Dying a new death
I said "*Hi Kailey*"
Sympathetically and for the first time she raised
her head
"*Hi!*" She smiled
I smiled in return
Friendship can blossom
Despite Evil's run

A SIDE NOTE ON EDUCATION

Learning more
Is making me *dumb*
And the excellence of yesterday years
Has started to really haunt

The purpose is to learn
The skills to which
One must earn
A living

Social distractions aplenty
Must be warred against
Here is a lesson
That to live in this world

You must understand well

It's high time to learn
The **masks** of life
To *grin*, to **laugh**
To *hope*, to **smile**.

And it will never do
To give in to turmoil
Skippity Skip
Heartbeats toil
So, keep the rhythm youthful
Don't recoil
From reason.

It's wonderful to love
My daily tasks
To go and learn
The trade to earn
Wisdom, not just of mind
But of the heart

It's time to learn
Priorities
Silly girl, she does not see
Past all the liberties
Her mirage of youth cages her

And the crescendo of ages
Will last till the date
Her routine depends on kissing perfection

So, let's play
These dumb charades
Where I own
What my face shows
Hide those treacherous tears
Don't let them flow
Don't be a fool
People have other things to do

And *silly silly* girl
Don't play the fool
Beyond your nest
Stakes are high
Every day is a quest
Concentrate on being the best

And if I am here to learn
That I'll ace
So what if today failed?
Embarrassment has its own lessons
Don't skip a day
Be brave
Create

Poetry from Pain

My pen draws blood
That looks like words
And my family does not like
The depth of its red

Too sad, too morbid, too painful, is the page
They wouldn't associate
Me without solace

They don't like the thought
Of bleakness in the world
Created for their child by them

But my heart, it bleeds if it keeps
Too much heaviness
It does grow blunt
As my pen sharpens
And I feel free that a future reader has heard
Already my cries through my silent struggle
It gladdens this vain mind that I am not alone
The mind of a reader
 Is time travelling backward
And is right here with me

I feel your presence

In this dark endeavour
And I am crazy to find it illogical
If somebody could doubt the veracity of these
intuitions

And to the nurturer is my following woe:

There is no safe space to rant
Why do you think the worst of me?
Why do you think I'm bad?

Jealousy and evil and ugliness
A soulless pretty gal

I am but a reflection
Of your insecurities

You can excuse your own slips
But remember my sorry deeds

Why do you preach positivity?
Practice what you preach

Remember that time you screwed
At others nosy treats

I am not going to be fine
Following you ideals
But I'll be the perfect Dame

Being myself for me

As I yearn for you to

This bird has finally learnt
The bravest warriors fly solo
You were my safe space to rant
But *oh!* You judged me so

So keep your hoity principles
I don't care, no more

Why do you think I don't care
About your say-so

Humility does not suit me
The queen wasn't meant to serve

I am simply perfect
Unlike your uptight self

Why do you think I only feel,
Ungently to you favoured one
(S)he ain't that great
Unlike me who was meant to soar.

Good Girls Hate Trouble

He was a boy
And that was enough
For me to hesitate
Drinking in his company

A lifetime of rules
Would render it cruel
For disappointment of hopes pinpointed on me
To rage supreme
In actions and emotions

The stories are interesting
Each worse than the other
Of bets and cheating and two-faced whispers
That speak to tease of treachery and disgust
And I would hate it, hate it
If gossip percolates my name in its mixture

So much for caring about the view of the world
I have been taught to play
Only the game of being the good girl in this
society
And them butterflies, must be resisted killed,
and buried
I cannot afford to be led astray
It's trust issues and more than that

The fear of emotional tears

So when he said, "*hi*"
I read him as I had heard of him
Of his trail of women who fell in love
With his cute smile and curly hair
And his heart never beat enough
To let it belong to any One

And if nobody could
I sure as hell was not enough
To keep him to me
I could not understand
the Speciality

So I said a polite hello
But his closeness was ignored
Or rather pushed away
Because I was afraid to want more

I would be loathe to be
A part of floozies
That the men loved hearing about
Tongue lashing of women qua women
And they enjoyed
Mirage of their unity
As the girls laid their secrets bare

They were ever too ready to lend an ear

Only to make it a meme
In their personal sphere
And the girls unassuming would dance it out
Without acknowledging reality
Hoping they were the specialty (unique)

So, I kept my distance
And eventually interest faded away
He said "*hi!*", to another girl
And raised his eyebrow that way
My heart forever would lurch at his actions
And my crush would remain
Unspoken of
Not even he knew
But I always wondered
What would have been
If I had held out my hand
And let him caress
My fingers as he reached out to me

On Friendship

To find friendship in a soul you always thought
Was unsalvageable in its very existence
Much has been written about
The butterflies that romance raises
But what about the moths of friendship?

And I was finally reveling
The fact that all the pacts
That had existed in my seclusion
Had culminated in me forming one of my own
Friendships to last
Battles fought
And our own Mecca was protected in unity

So now when questions prodded
About her mythical boyfriends
I defended
When she screamed as she was
Easily ignited
I protected her from the world of hate

I believed the tales
And had heard whispers
That found me annoying
And I was insecure enough
To worship somebody who didn't

So I stood up for her
During lectures
She was mean to teachers and bad with numbers
I stood by her
When she missed her classes
She was lazy in existence, a wasted spot

And slowly I began
Drowning in that one security
She was my secret keeper
And I told her a lot
More than I had any right to
There are secrets belonging to
Singular souls constituting the self

And the more I told her
The more dependency grew
To keep her tied
So she does not spew
My realities...

A BREAK IN CHRONOLOGY

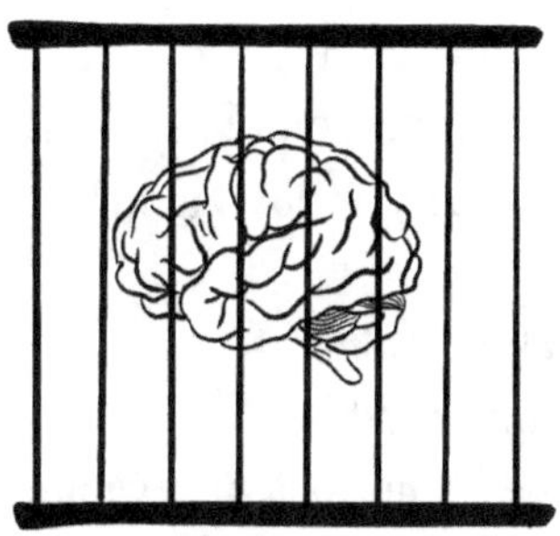

The effects of all that is laid
Were felt deeply
Long too
As longings subdued
Into to cynical hatred (of the world and oneself)

Its wonderful to see me
Reflected with a smile
And I wave my hand up
Synchronized
The smiling eyes look at me
And I greet myself
"hello old friend"

It took me seven years
As my madness started to ease
And I could get over
All past misdeeds

The hurt from friendly fire
Is still not completely healed
But the scars are good
And the experience, sound
There is **Victory** following my lead.

And my back is strong
And mind controlled
I've dispelled all notions of revenge and kind
But I am glad
I do not forget
Easily.

I questioned myself
When I was fine
The world was in the wrong
It takes courage to be yourself
When you're told you're not strong

I knew better as a toddler
Doing what I want
Not bending too much to the whims

There is a tiredness in my soul
That is leaching away from my dreams.
In the mirror of reality
There isn't much I want to see
And I want to scream like a diva and say-

Did you know?
That there was a queen next to you
You made her cry
Inside silently
You made her lonely
ToPsEy-TuRvEy
Her life goes jumping

In this world
I am all alone
Affection is all disguise
Acceptance is step one
To the road
To make myself smile

After all has been said and done
I find myself unable to ignore
The presence of those who in the past
Had touched my life, a memorabilia store
The past is in the past
Is it?
The only present today is haunted by the past
I don't want it to last
Because there is only hurt
And happiness digested well and did not leave
Lasting wounds to be remembered so vividly

And those that did

Have left a guilt
And made me feel
Less worthy of deserving
That one kind moment
For gratitude is a burden
I find it harder to bear than hatred.

Horror is in the aftermath

Of remembering embarrassment all night
I betray myself too quickly and fast
And silence is the response
And in silence I am hurt
Piercing the cocky self-assurance
No confidence to hold.

But wait a while
There is more
The tale has a few more doors

Why, Kailey?

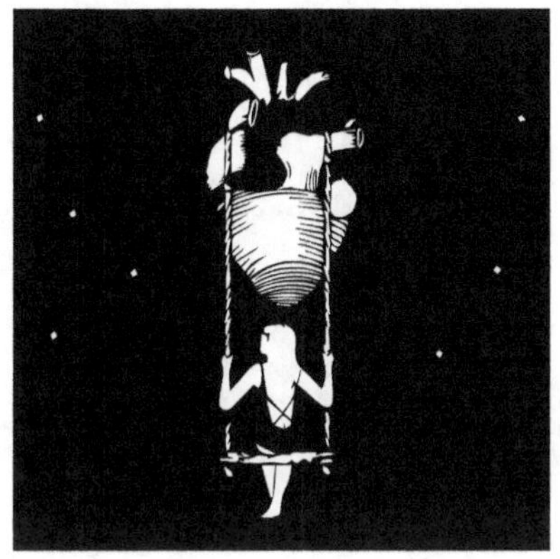

The problem began the day
I was laughing as I was talking
At the table with seven others
All silently watching
Me describe my day

And Kailey said, *"stop being annoying"*
And I found myself wanting to school the hurt
my face showed
Unendowed I remained as such talents eluded
me
I wanted to hate her
But ended up hating
Myself a little more
For staying silent

The others had that knowing look
Smugness of the one
Who had witnessed something morbidly
satisfying
Taking guilty pleasure
In watching firsthand
Some gross fun
Of which they were invisible participants.

We returned to the room
She did not apologise
I hate myself for not making her

She had that smile
Of power corrupted
That Tatsed delighted
And had her first sip of sadism

Our friends came
To the neighboruing door
And my shame
Amplified my hatred
In the next turn of events
(happening on that very day)

Kailey forgot her Wallet
Which she needed
As we sought to depart

To the supermart
So she snaps her fingers
And I (stupid? aye!)
Wagged my tail and followed her directions

The discomfort began growing
As the frequency of her lashing
grew more potent
The one fine day
I got a text
That showed how she had
Posted screenshots of our personal chats to
stories
Hiding my name
But making the form obvious
That anybody who knew
Could not be so naive not to recognise
And what's more delicious
Is those who mind
Know the extent to which
I have defendant her sorry deed

There's evil in her eyes
That I recognize
As the breadcrumbs of my life
Are swept by her mind
And recycled with embellishments
Fit for horrific retellings

All I want to know is why
Why did you do it?
What made you convince yourself
That I deserved that kind of hatred?
If you had to hate me then why did you befriend
me
In the first place
And why if you befriended me
Did you have to trick me, stab me, shame me
Blame it on your making
Escape the blame by faking
Love in friendship behind public eye
And if friendship is what you wanted
Why did you pick the band and drop it
And stabbed it under your big toe
When your eyes met my foe
Who you couldn't help but adore
Because you enjoyed someone massaging
That negativity you harbored from the get go
Against the first person who saw who gave a
damn (*that's me*)

Maybe the first impression isn't the last
impression
But one shouldn't forget that first vibe
They get from a person's smile,
Happy or just vile
Because when words flow
The sixth sense falls asleep (*doze*)

And yearning grows
To escape evil within
By allowing the benefit of the doubt
To swallow your instinct

I knew who you were the first time I saw you
I knew you well before you spoke
But I refused to believe
I had done such bad deeds
In the past to be stuck with
The person I suspected you to be

And you have done it now
Made me regret
Standing for a friend (*you*)
When the entire college
Called you a ****
Nitpicked every part of you
Spreading stories galore
And you have excelled impossibly
In making me ashamed
For standing up for a friend (*you*)
Who left me fighting her harassers
I would have still defended you
A woman for a woman
I would have still defended you
A person for one more
I regret helping you
the friends that

Used me as a wipe
To clean the bottom of her sole
I regret being a fool
For being emotional about a person like you

And every day I have woken up to the sound of
her texts
In my head
'St*u'

'Istg I'll smack u'
Beats me black and blue
The minutes my eyes close
But now its time to say goodbye
I wash your filth
Away from my mind
And am glad I met you
As I learnt to trust
Instinct
I learnt to have guts
Over security
And above all
Your only secret keeper will be family

A BROKEN MIND AND A SELFISH HEART

I'm sitting here
Stung by the memories that circle me
With sharks fins
They leap at me and try to drown
My sanity into my lack of will

And I am drawn by their negativity
It's a drug I love to hate
Those people whose existence I want to ignore
Exist completely to barb my mind
with past spoken words

Does it haunt them?
Their words uncalled for

I don't want to be her
With the mind poisoned with hatred
Of those whom her eyes seek

People transform in the public eye
From promisors in emotional privacy
To parrots in the play of social comedy
Comfort in one
Is a precursor to spilling of words spewed
Foolish in the one who knows not
The listener of secrets is forever cruel

At the first sign of breakage
Vulnerability is exploited
And then while the wound is fresh
Snip! snap!
They don't care
Swish the scissors
Breaking away the bonds
And binding new

What is left behind
Is the graveyard of solace and mental peace
And *oh*! If I could
Go back and grow myself
A backbone
Then this self-hatred could be overcome
I hope I am

Better when you dear reader

Are going through the **'trauma'** of this drama

queen

Healing (in the process of...)

It's wonderful to see me
Reflected with a smile
And I wave my hand up
Synchronized
The smiling eyes look at me
And I greet myself
"hello old friend"

It took me seven years
As my madness started to ease
And I could get over
All past misdeeds

The hurt from friendly fire
Is still not completely healed
But scars are good
And experience sound
There is Victory following my lead.

And my back is strong
And mind controlled
I've dispelled all notions of revenge and kind
But I am glad
I do not forget
Easily.
I questioned myself

When I was fine
The world was in the wrong
It takes courage to be yourself
When you're told you're not strong

I knew better as a toddler
Doing what I want
Not bending too much to the whims

There is a tiredness in my soul
That is leaching away from my dreams.
In the mirror of reality
There isn't much I want to see
And I want to scream like a diva and say-
Did you know?
That there was a queen next to you
You made her cry
Inside silently
You made her lonely
ToPsEy-TuRvEy
Her life goes jumping

In this world
I am all alone
Affection is all disguise
Acceptance is step one
To the road
To make myself smile

After all has been said and done
I find myself unable to ignore
The presence of those who in the past
Had touched my life, a memorabilia store
 the past is in the past

Is it?

The only present today is haunted by the past
I don't want it to last
Because there is only hurt
And happiness digested well and did not leave
Lasting wounds to be remembered so vividly
And those that did
Have left a guilt
And made me feel
Less worthy of deserving
That one kind moment
For gratitude is a burden
I find it harder to bear than hatred.

So every day for a year
I woke up with a bleeding heart
Scraped all night with memories bygone (*at last!*)
And every day for a year
I lived my worst moments
Chiding me. For not standing up
Banshees screaming in my year
The scream turned coherent

Into words that have already struck
Ugly faceless friends
(*out for blood*)
Morph into known ones, so detested
And my mind is infested
With a victim bug
Churning with hatred.

I get drunk with just how smart I am
And that is the stupidest attitude
 my mouth runs on emotions
With words dancing to its delight
Horror is in the aftermath
Of remembering embarrassment all night
I betray myself too quickly and fast
And silence is the response
And in silence, I am hurt
Piercing the cocky self-assurance
No confidence to hold.

THE UNCERTAINTY OF THE FUTURE

Some days feel mellow
When anger is done knocking on the mind's
door
It is fine to be walking
All alone
But in the line of fire
Shivers are made of uncertainties

And what is my disease?
What's decided in a group
Is not spoken out loud
And every day I'm slipping before the jury
I'd rather stay silent
I'd rather stay quiet
Sush and do what I'm told
Nothing more

All I want is to do well
In the few tasks that chose to dwell
In my company
But what to do
What are the rules
What's is obvious to the world
I'm learning slowly
Awkward like an old man
Hopping without a stick

Shy like a hatcheling
Biting to avoid being hit
Nervous like a tortoise
Being outrun by all hares
Cruel like Dumpella
Not getting out of Cinderella's hair
And now my resolve is shaking
Is there no hope
None at all
Oversmart would still only be wrong
Maybe I'm not smart at all

Beyond the classroom door

I wish there was a pill
To dissolve my introversion
I feel like a fish without gills
Praying silently for a diversion

I hesitate, swimming in my shyness
Painfully strong is the affliction
To hide from anger, to hide from kindness
And there is no book
Not even Carnegie
To tell me how to open up
To people around me
There is always a barrier
Between me and the world
And the weirdness in me dances to the tune of
bashful emotions

I wish I could do my work
Stay with my books
Talk to the world
About the world in the books
And I want nothing else
But to excel
It's making friends that hurts
Nothing new
I have quite a few

And they've been that way for ages
I'm *terrified* of letting slip
Every word in mind through my errant lips
And why does the world have it so easy
This art of conversation of nothing

Small talk is something
I never thought I'd need to survive
And I never know
Sometimes people talk in a flow
And other times I don't know whether to greet
If I say hello
They might retreat
And this profession is one I love
But the corollary of who to be
Someone liked
Someone easy
Is hurting my chances of progress
What do I do
There is no formula
I like myself but maybe there is something
wrong

Something I need to change
But whom do I talk to
I don't go beyond a hi
Everyone has a professional disguise
And I either open up fully or not at all
This balance is needed to achieve

Escape being crass
Hit the right spot
Of friendliness and self-respect
But what I really like
Is the quiet of my office
The solitude of noise
Of unread words

I wish I could stay
And read and inhale
All those phrases calling to me
But everything is a choice
Soft copies feel dishonest
And all I want to do is sit and relax and read till
I know
More than before
More than the author, more than a soul
But that is impossible
For everyone had a niche
And I am fledgling
Too far behind to catch up

I wish I could enjoy communications as much
There is no comfort
But always the pressure of being liked
I want to be but who am I?
Nobody, just a silly being
Hiding out and biding
Time to be like the greats I walk to the hall with

But greatness requires friendship
It took me enough time to open up to those
around
How will I speak to the world at large
When all I want is a **bookish pause**

The perils of a smile

The king too is only a pawn
In the chess player's hand
He is to be protected
Weak in the position
Of power
Lusted after
And in his names
All deeds she does
The queen

A pawn can evolve
If the player can solve
Its way to end
But which one to strategise about
Which one to leave
A game of conviction

A hand by the little one
Yearning to be suitably placed
Among its multiple twins
Not left to chance
No politics of demand
Just sweet pleadings
To escape its nothings
No embellishments
no tricks
Except to kill
With slanted moves
It's just a dance,
To anothers' beat

Both the queen and **pawn** face each other
And smile in greetings
Even words wear clothes
Meant to coax
Social standards to ward off weirdness
But which is which
That is the task
Am I the queen
Am I the **pawn**?
Am I neither
Only the sweeper
Positioned here to clean off blood
After the battlefield

Since that day when maturity hit

I began preferring
Anger over wit
Weed out the harmful funny bones
They are distraction before the magician
Pulls the rug from underneath
Sigh! The world is blistered, is hazy
And my teeth show my incompetence
Don't be foolish
Brutality is the weapon
The only one for survival

A LITTLE KIND

Careful when you let free words
From your lips,
Wings sprout they turn into birds
And perch
Into ears you wouldn't dream of
With every new branch
They are transformed
Into *snakes*, **wasps** and <u>beetles</u>
That eventually crawl back to you
And you detest the creatures that took birth
From the womb of your own emotions

In search of the deeper meaning
I forgot the route to the shore
The basics faded out
Leaving me drowning even at the shallows
And its bitter pill to be swallowed
That I have let the waves by

I looked at the mirror so long
For a validation
That the mirror started to look back
It put thoughts in my head
That could paint the day
As glorious or just sad

Look at that reflection and be a little kind
Give a shy shake of that hand
To yourself be polite
You are fine not as bad
As you think yourself to be
You will cope
You will make your own boat
In muchness you must believe

FOR TODAY YOU MUST LEARN

There's nothing I want more
Than my teachers' pride
I work because I'd like to
Be better, imbibe
Skill, morality and diligence
All I did was try
To work like I was taught
A hiccup, nay a disaster
Has made it seem like condemnation
Of my teachers' efforts

And I really wish you'd tell me
All my ugly truths
What haunts me is the finality
That the disappointment that hit the roof
Has cemented into permanence

Even if things stand
To this deadly stillness
Maybe one day it'll be seen
I wasn't completely a waste of time

My own gains have been huge
My **knotted tongue** has finally
Caught up with my brain

Maybe soon my speech will flow
Like the linguistics of my thoughts

What do I say
I did not speak
For three years before I leaped blind
Into a Hunger Games of orators
I know I know I like this game
Of warring words
It's **sublime**
But only because repeatedly
I was given a chance to better my being
That I inched toward my potential
I did not speak I did not talk I lamented my
shadow self
Three years stretched to a lifetime
I was born again

Those three years
All I did was write
And ink that bled on pages
Was held to produce beauty
But in my stillness
I kept catching my breath
Unable to release
Slowly and steadily
My speech deflated

Deep breaths I told myself
Anyways you won't last two days
Deep breaths I told myself
Anytime beyond that would be magic's way

And then I got to write
And although not very well
It was such a relief
To find some joy
In the pool of nervousness

For my heart would beat fast all-day
I was out in the world again
I had to talk
And force myself
To produce words that could count as
conversation

And it was easy for my mind
To grasp it all
But to force the words
Took practice
I felt like me again

My prayers had come true
For ever since I was a young girl
I prayed I could read and write for the rest of my
life

Funny how things turn out
I am where I am meant to be
And maybe one day
It will be seen
She was alright
Not a pimple
Out of place
Maybe it'll be okay
I'm better because I got to stay

WIDE EYES LOOK TO THE SOUL

I did not per se err
But compatriots are going down
And it feels like friendly fire
What really pinches is the knowledge
That we are grossly segregated
Three of us are crosses
And only one, a complete whole
I thought every bond was unique
To each his own
But knowing what I know
That every cough of mine
Is communicated in a jiffy
To one I thought was one of us

But seems like that has never been
Our negatives are told
To him with longevity,
I am drowning from my smiles
That in my memory hate me
Smiling and crying alike
Are weaknesses to exploit
And strengths to overcome...

To Err is Human

Nonsense, my mind
Strains to clear warring thoughts
And my choked hand clogs
In illustrating truth on the blank sheet

Blank because I am limited
Not the paper
Limited in the quickness
Of the profession decorated by many greats
Who are all turning in their graves

To have slipped by a folly
That disgraces childhood discipline
Vow to protect
Punctuality against tardy sins

Respect is not to be compromised with
There is a limit to tolerated
Inexperienced blabber
Vow to forge ahead
Vow to upkeep
Your life learnings
Against your sorry deeds

I'M ALRIGHT

The mistake was grave
Disproportionate brunt
Is heavy on one

Not so bad the
Don't cock up every day
The defence was belated in coming my way

I'm alright
I'm blessed by the stars
I'm alright
I belong in the hall
Of the worthy

Perception has magnified the error of one
It's in the past my mistakes they say
My mistakes are no greater than others on the
same page

I'm alright
My progress vast
I'm alright
I'm on the right path

The error is not denied

But the repercussion
The denial
Of the hard work put in
Bleeds the heart

And my clarity is unblemished
The first words that I spoke
Were through and through
True to core
Worthy of quotation untarnished
What was asked for
I furnished

I'm alright
My explanations sound
I'm alright
I will not be error-bound

Utterance is necessary
When pointed out
I'm good I'm sound
Don't have a problem
Mound

And there are things I too am better at
Keep going
There's light
At the end of the tunnel
(*Maybe sunshine too*)

I'm alright
Diligent to core
I'm alright
My work is good

I'm alright
I've seen the crowd
I'm alright
Lie through their teeth
Caught and expound
And yet they aren't considered
To err

The pattern in the same
The brunt is on me
Shut your emotions
Don't weep
Accept not what you aren't
I'm alright
True at least
Honest to my work
Painting good deeds

THIS BLASPHEMOUS INSECURITY

Some terrors ache beyond the soul
What do I say to make it more
Bearable to endure this void
The world was a playground and every error
Was a homework's reprimand
And now the responsibility has reared its head
For the first time
I wonder how to earn

How to sustain beyond trivial existence
Two days have punched the life
Two days of delight

Birthed a **boogeyman**

That's haunting me day and night

There's no escape
This prison of a vacation
Is spent strategising a gamble
If it stays then how long
Will this hollow horror be
Will it stretch for months and months
Forcing me to cease to be

Running away will not resolve
Repenting is the only salve
But punishment is in uncertain terms
What do I do?
I want to learn

And all the mirages of dreams have dissolved
Leaving behind pure reality
I see the world I could not before
The world of `clockwork beings`

Two days two days two days
The puppeteer has prepared his guillotine
The rope is pulled and the barrel falls
And I am afraid he won't stay stop

Narcissist

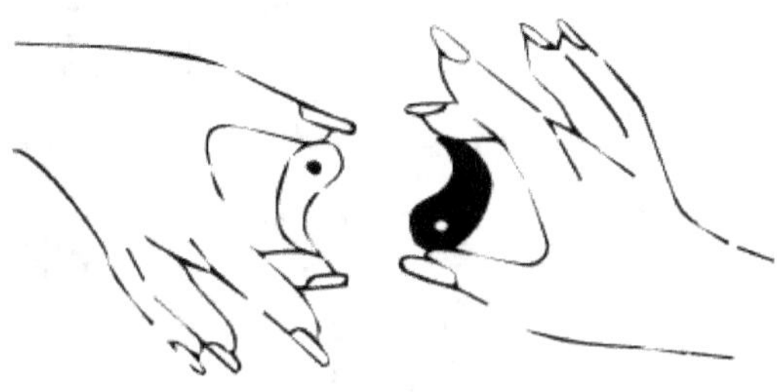

There is this jealousy deep inside
And instead of working
I whine
For the stars that elude me like my hard work
Why can't I
Embrace positivity and allow myself to lighten
This heart and float
Instead of drowning in all ugliness
Am I that bad?
Just coddle me and don't tell me to work
And don't tell me the truth
It's rather hurts
I hate I **hate** I **hate** this vibe
Kiss of the fairy
The demons smile

I Wish I was more

I guess I was wrong
I'm not mistaken
I had no wish
To speak before my brethren
I had no wish to speak at all
Had I not opened my lips
It would have been 'him' at fault
And from our end it was empty

The angry decision maker was already targeting
all that is tardy
Though I helped him he's made me his enemy
He pushed me into the fire
And all ends are loosening
What is worse that it's a downhill battle
It's been a month now
There is no hope
Of betterment
Nobody will tell me to leave
Three years
Will collapse into months

It was bad luck
What else is there to say

You leave me to vices and tell me then it's ok
And there's no fire no hope now
I fear the decision has been made
Even if I stay
There will be double to prove now
I know they ardently wish me away
And what is worse than being screamed at
Is being told I'm useless

The innuendo has come up too often to be
ignored now
In this world specifically is too stupid
And I'm aware of all that passes internally
There is an order in loudspeaker
Telling all she's not ready
And they would all be too happy to get someone
they want
Should I say goodbye
Or stay for now?

Swallow that bitter pill

Some days feel mellow
When anger is done knocking on the mind's
door
It is fine to be walking
All alone
But in the line of fire
Shivers are made of uncertainties

And what is my *disease*?

What's decided in a group
Is not spoken out loud
And every day I'm slipping before the jury

I'd rather stay silent
I'd rather stay quiet
Sush and do what I'm told
Nothing more
All I want is to do well
In the few tasks that chose to dwell
In my company
But what to do
What are the rules
What's is obvious to the world

I'm learning slowly
Awkward like an old man

Hopping without a stick
Shy like a hatcheling
Biting to avoid being hit
Nervous like a tortoise
Being outrun by all hares
Cruel like Dumpella
Not getting out of Cinderella's hair
And now my resolve is shaking
Is there no hope
None at all
Oversmart would still only be wrong
Maybe I'm not smart at all.

The Balm Is In Your Blood

Smile at yourself
Laugh in your company
Fight with your fears
Then take a deep breath and step out
Let the real world begin

Smile through injustice
Laugh through pointed glares
Then take a deep breath and swallow
Your remarks that you wish to share

Smile and write your own story
Laugh as you work hard
Then take a deep breath and inch
Towards the future where you can be yourself

Oversmart

Here, I am reaping what I've sowed
I've enjoyed delegated comfort
Swimming in bliss
Unbeknownst to the flowing responsibility in titbits
Carefully, **carefully** I must wade
Every aspect or dig my grave
Each task outsourced
Will come back to bite me more
My ivory tower is cracking
The gratefulness which was in me lacking
Has turned to inefficiency
And each task must be neatly sewed
And close with perfection of a solid needle stick
What of law when I can't manage
Nuggets in this humongous whole

This One for Anger

What's funny is the story of the bootlicker
With gutter in his mind
He was scared for his lying god
To disapprove of his behind
Faceless he's finally in the room
He'll evaporate for approval
For he wishes to be groomed
To clean well his master's shoes
Gutter, did you say
You (*not so little*) little fool

My first retort was one too good
But spoken out loud and not resisted
I'm not weak, I don't inhale the weed
My flattery grows, choking me from inside
That old liar, he dares throw me into the fire
For the third time
But there is still dignity of the one fighting
The bootlicker though
With no mind of his own
Wags his tail and licks on
He's already lost
I'm only battle worn

As I Look Back

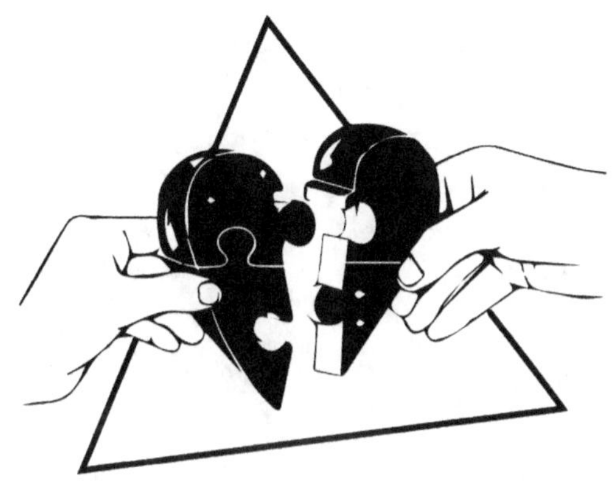

𝓗𝓪𝓾𝓷𝓽𝓲𝓷𝓰𝓵𝔂 comical

Is the fragility of a begginer's situation
To hope to grow
And then be shown
That downfall is right next door

Every morn's prayer was
God! I hope I do an honorable job
And my hope hurts
And the hope in me
looks at me at home and wonders
What is wrong
Why does she not
Go as she did to learning's abode?

Dignity belongs to us all
Tall or short, big or small
If lopsided the situation be now
A status quo redefined
I have given up my heroic dreams
What will not change
Is my silly speech
Burnt to history

Oh, but if I could
Give an arm
Turn back the clock and shut my mouth
Maybe we would be alright
Everything would be just divine
And as salt spills to mouth
And sleep comes earlier than nine
There is no hope I know that now
But I'll be fine
I'll be fine

Oz

If only I preferred
Reading more about the world that exists
Than the world of *"princesses and pirate ships"*
Would I be better? Smarter? Sharper?
Could I keep my mind
Without flying to Oz?
Could I keep on talking
As discussions chalk out,
History and law and foreign affairs?

Conversations are now
Shy of abstract
It's a game of mining
Words from words
Emotions adorn
Things, not set in stone
Perhaps that will never haunt
Reality

Am I too **weird**?
For this world
I belong too much to my thoughts
And the happenings around me
Are imagined realities
Shaded with a hue of fantasy

Now and then
I get a dose
And jarred by truth
I am forced to ignore
The call of the great authors that make my world

And better friends
I dare you to find
They are me and mine
Alone in this arena
Of checkers

But who am I
If not a little mad
Some things are powers
Not weaknesses dismissed
Cry through the world
But do not miss
Your individuality lies in your imaginary kin

A DESERT LIKE MEMORY

Honour me good
Dear books as I say
Hola! *Salut*! *Hello*! And *Namaste*.

Beyond the greetings is Chapter 1
The grip on my mind is glorious fun
Who am I?
In the reader's zone
All are down
with the fun fever
Of main character syndrome

And shyly, shyly
I experience in real
Second-hand embarrassment
That makes me snap shut the pages and giggle

And the heroes
Brave of heart
Become me and I start
Knocking away enemies with my sword (gifted
by the Gods).

A **crash**! A **bang**!
A hoo! A ha!
Suddenly I realise
I've broken a vase
And the warrior is snatched away from my soul
As my mother's footsteps come closer to the
door.

And dear me!
My sword (a broom) gets snatched from me
Down goes the warrior
To reality

HOME

Poke a toe out
Let the cold in
Sneakily sneakily
through the slit
A steaming mug along with
Mother's kiss
Added is the comfort of hot chocolate
Outshadowing all guilt

Warmth knitted
Through loving hands
That still cradle
My inner child
A little bit of sunshine
Curtsy emotional charm

It's a wonderful winter morning
Take a deep breath
Let the cold sing
And dance to the lullaby
Of bare branches swinging

Don't hush
Even nature yells
Joy is for perspective to derive
Fun is in the smell
Of wood fire
And camping with friends

Remember the holes in your gloves
Have their own worth
The flavour of the season
Is through all five senses

Getting Better

There's a *giggle* in me
I wish to cease
As I grow a tad old
I wish I could dance differently
Before family and outside folk

Why do I say
My mind too soon
Why can't I know who to be
Questions that ought not to plague
Past teenage years, smear
My mind too much too often

And all the glee
Is a waste as I
Take one step forward then jump back three

There is no consistency
No rhythm of an upward graph
Around me, everyone perfectly grows better
And all I do is laugh

I miss the gifts I was born with
A memory astonishingly eidetic
It still greets me in bouts

That renders me ecstatic

Giggle giggle
The issue lies

Giggle giggle
Not in comprehension

Giggle giggle
I was used to being

Giggle giggle
The centre of academic attention

To be reborn vide
A discipline
I vowed to never return to

And therein lies the issue
The tongue speaks silly
When the brain doubts
A nugget of a comprehensive whole.

To learn something is to know it full
A single doubt leads to cruel
Stammering and hesitation and repeated
questioning
This isn't the 'me' I know.

But laugh silly
Laugh and roll
The world walks on, glorious

A text that lacks grace from the start
Is banished from visuality
And I cannot see the path of reasoning
Joining points of understandability
Only if I get all the answers in one
No doubt that presses a corner cone
Quickly do my fingers fly
Answering all textual whys

It's easy but I can't help
Now and then a silly spell
What to do
Will I last?
I want to but without my laugh

Then again my mother says
Be yourself, not anyone else
But being myself is being silly these days
Everyone else gets the game
how many chances will I get?
Till someone pulls the plug and says
That's enough of you! **We cannot tolerate**!
You and your detestation gaze.

Yet there is tomorrow

The most wonderful thing
Adorning sunshine with opportunities
Nothing grand but a will to be
Better understandably

Every pigeon was born to fly

There once was a pigeon
Who could not fly
While her sisters cried joyously
As the winds sang a tune and swept them such
They flew around in glee.

Six months (*yes, full six*)
She could not even flap
Harder she tried
Worse she failed
Her faith begun to snap

Her limits were in a deeper pit
Than others in her space
That just meant that her leap (*when she did*)
Would be longer than her kin

There is a strange affliction
Some have when they are pushed
Into the grand arena
Of uncharted newness

To know completely or not at all
Are binaries that exist
When flapping away from a cliff
No mid-way exists

So the pigeon went to her nest
And practiced in seclusion
She read and wrote and learnt from observation
And formulated her own version

And it took a lot of midnight labour
To stabilize her betterment
But pigeons are as pigeons do
And every future is a quest.

www.ingramcontent.com/pod-product-compliance
Lightning Source LLC
LaVergne TN
LVHW011016200726
843509LV00011B/1130